God's Polished Arrows

The Story of Frank and Betty Clarke and Their Work Amongst the Lani People of West Papua

By Frank Clarke

Edited by Joseph Stephen

ISBN: 978-0-9944042-3-7

Special thanks to Joseph's wife, Mary Stephen who was the catalyst and bulldog at our heels to get this amazing testimony committed to paper, and who organized the numerous interviews, arranged the transcription of the notes, and kept on us until it was completed.

Special thanks to Corri-Jayne for transcribing dozens of recorded interviews into notes from which this manuscript was compiled.

Thanks to Wes Dale for helping bring some order from chaos as jottings in Frank's journals were in three languages, often with his own style of abbreviations. Many of the recorded interviews with Frank contained fragmented thoughts and memories which lacked context and dates.

Thanks to Steve Solomon who designed this book and did the typography and final copy editing. Thanks also to Gerard Wilson who helped with transcribing hand-written journals, scanning slides, and labelling photos.

Special thanks also to Biz Adams, Desley's daughter (Frank and Betty's grand daughter) for the cover design. The cover photos were taken by Dave Martin on a trip he did with Frank Clarke.

Disclaimer

This book was compiled in Frank's final two years from many personal interviews and from handwritten journals. We have done our best to ensure correct chronology and detail. If errors are discovered with dates, names, or timeframes, we apologize.

Contents

Foreword	by Desley Parsons (Nee Clarke)	5
Chapter 1	My Childhood and Conversion	9
Chapter 2	Preparation and Calling	11
Chapter 3	First Impressions	15
Chapter 4	First Posting Mamit	25
Chapter 5	Resistance of the Yali Tribe	45
Chapter 6	Tragedies and Trials	51
Chapter 7	Communicating the Gospel	55
Chapter 8	Daily Dealings	61
Chapter 9	Our Second Post - The Lakes Plains	69
Chapter 10	Vet, Surgeon, Dentist and More	73
Chapter 11	Evangelism in the Lakes Plains Area	79
Chapter 12	Later Years	83
Chapter 13	My Last Visits	89
Conclusion		94
Postscript	by Joseph Stephen	96

Foreword
(by Desley Parsons, the oldest daughter of Frank and Betty Clarke)

My father Frank and mother Betty began a pioneer work which became part of a mighty movement of God throughout the central highlands of what is now known as Papua.

Over the years Dad had many and varied roles—learning the language, community development, literacy development, field chairman of the mission, development of the local indigenous church and their ministry to further tribes and helping to establish a Bible school for them. Dad seemed to be on a mission throughout his life to make life easier for himself and others in whatever way he could. He built proper roads around the mountainous area of Mamit so that he could more easily visit the outlying villages for ministry and medical help. He introduced rabbits and fishponds to add more protein to the diet of the villagers; he was an early adopter of any technology that may be useful. He was the man you went to if you wanted something fixed or invented. Many a mission family were thankful to Frank each time they had a warm shower. He loved these people like his own. And they loved him. These people became his second tribe.

Mum left school at twelve and went to work on a homestead because the family moved and there was no room for her to go with them. It was four years before she was able to join them in their new house. This time was valuable as it put her in contact with a woman who nurtured and discipled Betty into becoming the disciple of Christ who would end up in a remote village in the mountains of

Netherlands New Guinea with her husband, a young boy and being heavily pregnant. Although she never claimed to be a teacher—and readily admitted to not being able to cope with the demands of home schooling using correspondence lessons—we remembered what we had learned from her—the love of books, the playing on the little pedal organ, and learning to sew on the old singer treadle sewing machine.

The girl who only went to school until she was twelve never stopped learning. She went on to study nursing and midwifery. Then she went to a Bible College and then to Linguistics training. All with the aim of becoming a missionary nurse.

As a child growing up in the mountain village where the only contact with the outside world was via the two way radio and the Cessna aircraft that brought mail, food and medical aid or took us out to other places, this was all very natural. After all, I was born here in this village and my brother was too young to remember anything else. Because I have become a mother myself and then revisited that village after many years of living in civilization, I have become amazed at what my mother had done. She packed up all her belongings and boarded a ship bound for Hollandia with Dad and a three month old baby and then was flown in a little tin box with wings into the mountainous interior of a strange land where men wore gourds and women wore strings. She learned a language that was only just being written down. She was the medical expertise where there was nothing else! She raised a family in a village where there were no other English speaking people and taught literacy to adults who had never even seen a pencil or book. She trekked the mountains and valleys to provide medical aid and to bring the good news of Christ. The nearest doctor was only available during daylight hours via radio when they had medical needs of their own. Talking on the radio was not easy for mum because all radio traffic was in Indonesian.

She was separated from her own mother and father by thousands of miles, no phones, no internet, just snail mail. When her own father passed away she could not be with her mother.

Once the language had been learned and accommodation made a bit nicer with the building of a new house, things must get easier. Right? Wrong! The children were getting to school age. That's ok. There is such a thing as correspondence lessons. But how do you keep the children focused on lessons when their Dani friends are eager to distract them away down the airstrip for ball games. Rainy days were no better because playing in the overflowing ditches was just as attractive.

Over the next few years mum suffered severe burns from a kerosene cooker and had several miscarriages. Furloughs meant lots of travelling around visiting supporting churches and family—or being left alone with the children while Dad was travelling. When we returned to the mission field, saying goodbye to family was difficult as she wondered if she would ever see them again.

There are many more memories that we could talk about—how she could turn from being afraid of that little bull into a lioness protecting her young when the little one was threatened by it. To move from being the district nurse to being the hostess for all who visited the mission and to all new missionaries. To having to leave children behind in Australia (and they were not good at writing).

As we contemplate the life of Betty, we are also acknowledging that she was never able to do these things in her own strength. She was not adventurous, she was not brave. She was quiet and reserved and did not like crowds. Whatever she did in her life she did because of her love and commitment to her Lord and Saviour. As she stepped out in faith, she was given strength, comfort, ability and perseverance to "run the race that was set before her". Being a missionary is not glamorous. Being a missionary does not make you a super Christian, but the only way to make it, is to truly rely on God—it's not just a catch phrase. It's a way of life.

Mum and Dad, we see you both as God's polished arrows, used mightily in his purpose, dearly loved by two tribes, one family. The family of God.

Chapter 1 - My Childhood and Conversion

I was born on the 18th of January 1934 at Moltema, a small rural hamlet on the outskirts of Elizabeth Town in Tasmania. I had eight brothers and sisters, there were nine of us altogether. My mother died before I was two years of age. Dad remarried when I was four. His second wife had four children. In my childhood, and growing up I was belittled and made to feel inferior. I grew up with lack of confidence. My father used to call me names and my stepmother even queried my sanity. It wasn't until the Lord got hold of me that I was able to accept myself as I am.

Like many young boys, I did not enjoy school. I would much rather be outdoors. I would observe ants, birds, rabbits and other animals for hours. I figured out that bad weather was imminent when the ants started cleaning out their anthills and bringing out the sand. Rabbits usually foraged at night, so when I observed them coming out to feed at 10 in the morning I also learned that it would be a rough evening. I noticed how plovers, whose eggs were almost invisible, located their own nests in the open field. I observed that they first located a nearby landmark. Our property had a little creek running through it where I would play and often catch small eels. Our family enjoyed eating them.

When I was twelve, we moved to Hagley. I learned to tickle trout. When we used to go to the lakes in the highlands of Tasmania I would feel under the banks for them and slowly and gently caress them until they were used to my touch. Once it was accustomed to my touch I'd then grab the trout by the gills and thus procure dinner.

I marveled at the innate knowledge and skill that animals seemed to possess. Because of my study of animals my parents called me the grand title of professor Pig-Dung Expert.

I withdrew into myself. From the age of 14 to 19 I hardly spoke to anyone. I was just an angry young man. I didn't talk to anyone. I just loved being outdoors away from people.

At Hagley, we attended the Methodist Church and I went to Sunday School. When I was about 14 a travelling evangelist visited the area. I responded to the appeal to give my life to the Lord Jesus. I went forward because his message was compelling. I thought I was a Christian because I'd made a mental decision. The local minister heard about it and he accepted me into the Methodist church as a member. Then I was able to participate in the Lord's Supper but life just went on, nothing really changed in me.

At the age of 21 I went to Victoria to work in Forestry. Our team of men would clean up the remaining branches and stumps after the loggers had been through. These leftovers were used for pulp wood in paper making. I used to travel from the bush into the city to my uncle Lionel and aunt Amy's place. My uncle was an ex-Salvation Army Officer and a keen Christian. He would take me to Ringwood Gospel Hall with him on Sunday mornings. I would partake of the Lord's Supper. One day he asked me about my salvation. Because I gave him such a vague answer of my conversion he sent me some gospel tracts and insisted I read them carefully. He told me he was concerned about my understanding of what it meant to be a Christian.

One morning, on the 25th of September 1956, in the tin shed in the bush where I was living, having read the tracts, I was convicted of my sin. I knelt down next to my bed on the dirt floor and I prayed. The mental profession all those years ago finally became a heartfelt conviction. That morning, the Lord gave me assurance of my sins forgiven, filled me with joy and peace and I knew I had eternal life. I was almost 23 years old.

Chapter 2 - Preparation and Calling

I had a desire to go overseas and be a missionary from the time of my conversion in September, 1956. I had a battle however with that because the devil was tempting me; I thought that I may have had to stay at home. With the Lord's help I won the battle in my mind and heart. I was wanting to go, but just always stopped. The Methodist church had a local meeting but they were lacking preachers so they asked me to stay at home and be a preacher. Dad had to leave the farm because of bronchitis. Out of necessity and filial piety I thought that I might have to work the farm. Other members of the family, however, were available to take care of the farm, freeing me up to go.

By February, 1957, I was undertaking a two-year Bible course at the Melbourne Bible Institute. Every Monday morning a missionary would come and speak of their missionary work. They lectured for about an hour. Over the 2 years I heard about 60 missionaries from different places speak about their work. This gave us a great exposure to world missions.

The group of young people I was part of were focused on Nepal because it had just been opened up to the gospel so initially I was interested in going to Nepal. The problem was that one had to go as a qualified tradesman—such as a butcher or builder so that we could pass on our skills to the locals—but I didn't have a trade.

My focus then turned to working in Papua because I'd heard a missionary talk about the change in the lives of the Lani people through hearing the word of God. This is where the Lord confirmed my appointment to Papua.

It was like a door opened and I walked through it.

While I was at the Melbourne Institute, I met my first wife, Betty McCrae. (Betty was born on the 31st of December 1932 in Wonthaggi Victoria.) When we finished studying we were married; this was on 25 July, 1959. Our theme verse was inscribed on her wedding ring which was Psalm 34:3 "O magnify the Lord with me and let us exalt his name together" KJV.

Paul Gesswein spearheaded Regions Beyond Missionary Union (RBMU) which was beginning to work in Netherlands New Guinea. We met with the RBMU Board and they appointed us to go to Papua as missionaries.

We attended the Summer Institute of Linguistic course in Victoria before we went. The course taught us how to write up a language and how to work on the grammar. We crammed into 11 weeks what normally would have been a year-long university course.

We had to wait in due process to get things in order. At that time they were going to have an American and Australian section of the mission in Papua. They needed an experienced missionary to go with us for the Australian section. They couldn't send me, just a raw recruit, so we had to wait until a suitable missionary could be found.

Finally, they found a family, Stan and Pat Dale, who had been missionaries in Papua New Guinea. They were offered the position and accepted to go to Papua. We were also then free to go.

(Looking back, it was ironic that Stan was never actually appointed field leader but I was appointed to that position several times.)

By that time Betty was pregnant with our first baby. The women on the council insisted that we stay home for the birth of our first child—just as well we did as it was a difficult birth, a forceps delivery and then a retained placenta. If we had been on the field this would have spelt certain disaster.

Then our mission Regions Beyond Missionary Union decided to merge the Australian and North American sections under one leadership for simplicity. We were told of their decision just as we

Chapter 2 - Preparation and Calling

were about to depart, the delay in this deliberation was providential due to David's complicated birth. God's timing is always perfect.

David was born in Shepparton, Victoria on the 6th of May 1960. When he was 4 months old we were allowed to travel.

We went on a boat called the Sinabang. This was a cargo boat with 16 cabins. The full circuit of the boat was from the western coast

David about age 1 and Frank

of Australia, around the south of Australia, then up the east coast, up to and around the islands and back to its starting point on the west coast of Australia. The circuit took about three months. The boat did four circumnavigations a year.

The boat had travelled from Perth via the west coast of Australia and then to Melbourne where we boarded. Then it continued up to Sydney. We had a cabin to ourselves. When we arrived in Sydney we had to berth for a week due to a wharf workers strike. We stayed on the boat in Sydney for that week. On the three-week boat journey, each Friday morning, breakfast was a plate of raw mince, which you would eat with a spoon, mixed with raw egg (we skipped breakfast those days).

We went on our way up the Australian coast, then along the northern coast of New Guinea and finally to Hollandia, the capital of Netherlands New Guinea.

Chapter 3 - First Impressions

When we arrived at Hollandia we anchored outside the harbour overnight because we arrived there on Sunday and would have had to pay wharfage charges. The day we arrived was the 25th of September 1960, exactly four years after my conversion. We came ashore early Monday morning, the 26th of September and were met in Hollandia, the capital of Dutch New Guinea, (becoming West Papua, 40 years later,) by missionaries who travelled to meet us from where they were working in Sentani, where the main airport was located.

When the boat dropped us at Hollandia, I was looking out for

25 September 1960, arriving at the Port of Hollandia

snakes and looking at the soil. I thought in a different land that it would be different soil but the soil looked like that in Tasmania. The only difference was that there was a lot more jungle than in Tasmania—and there is a lot of forest in Tasmania.

After two weeks of orientation, we were flown in a Cessna 180 light aircraft to Karubaga. We took off at about 6:30 AM from Sentani on the coast. The pilot was Dave Stieger, a US airforce pilot during World War II, who became the field leader of Mission Aviation Fellowship in Dutch New Guinea. The flight took about 1 hour 20 minutes. The little Cessna 180 could carry five passengers and the pilot. I sat alongside the pilot and asked about the various controls. As we flew he gave a running demonstration of each control. One control made the tail wiggle, another made us suddenly ascend, then suddenly descend—to the horror of Betty who informed me that next flight I'd be sitting in the back with her.

We flew over what looked like a small saw tooth mountain range which was impassable by foot. We then flew over a swamp area crossing the Idenberg river, one of the major rivers of the region. The river looked like a big coiled up snake from the air. Finally we flew over a mountain pass at over 9,500 ft then descended into the valley at about 5,000 ft above sea-level where the Lani people we were going to work with lived. As we passed through the Toli valley their huts came into view, looking like mushrooms planted along the ridges. After a couple of turns to the left and to the right the Lani huts became more visible and I could see that they were made of split boards and grass thatched roofs.

As we came into land at Karubaga in the light aircraft it dawned on me that we were finally amongst the Lani people. We landed on the grass airstrip located at about 5,000 ft up on the side of the mountain taxiing in on an ax-head shaped parking area where we were met by a group of our first living real Lani people.

The women wore modest coverings of string skirts which covered the lower body only. The men were dressed in nothing but a genital

Mountainous view of Mamit looking toward the Wunin; Bokondini mountain pass to the east of Mamit

gourd and a net bag on their head to keep their hair in place. Some of the men's hair reached below their waist. The women had short hair. The men's long hair was meant to attract the women during their dancing rituals. The men would use pig fat in their hair to hold its shape. The bald men would pack their net with something to look like hair (usually grass, later when it became available, paper).

When they saw the photos that I sent home of the Lani men gathered around the airstrip where we landed my auntie and uncle made the comment that the men looked like they were armed with a cannon, referring to their 200-300 mm genital gourds.

I didn't feel as though I'd arrived until I reached Karubaga and was amongst the people. During our first two weeks at Hollandia and Sentani in West Papua we experienced much Dutch influence and met English-speaking missionaries. But the introduction to the Lani culture was rather confronting. There they were—men just wearing their genital gourd and women wearing only a grass skirt. Some missionaries had culture shock. I didn't, but it was different. They weren't like the missionary stories of these barbaric people that would kill you on sight, they were human beings. It didn't shock me—that's how they are and I'm here amongst them. And they were friendly.

When I arrived, I went into the jungle thinking that I had a superior, western education. I could read and write, operate

Lani tribal men 1961

machinery—modern machinery. I thought I was superior to them. I had read books on savages and thought that I'd be dealing with uneducated simpletons but I couldn't have been more wrong.

After living and working with them, seeing what they could do, I realized that they were both skillful and knowledgeable. Although they never attended school they had learned culturally appropriate life skills and environmental wisdom.

They had studied nature and they would have an equivalent of a university degree in forestry plus a university degree in something else. They had much natural knowledge that they would pass on from one to the other. I was walking through the forest one day asking about different trees, and they said, "If you show us a bit of leaf and a bit of bark, we will tell you the name of that tree." There were thousands of different types of trees and they could identify each one. Now, that's a lifetime of study. So these people were certainly ahead of me in local knowledge.

My first reaction was amazement. They were like stone-age people, still using stone age tools. They had stone axes and stone chisels that had been traded into the area, which they valued very much. Later on they would work 40 days for one steel axe. (We also purchased the land used for the airstrip and mission station with steel axes.)

Their culture was also seemingly more advanced in terms of self-governance. For example, consider their manners and courtesies. There was no centralized government but common law was practiced amongst the clans. Adultery was not accepted in marriage even though premarital relationships were accepted. One thing that amazed me was that you would go into a culture where there was no sense of "western" authority, no centralized government, yet if someone killed or harmed another person or when someone stole a pig from another clan, they would handle the crime in an orderly, just and acceptable manner. Decisions were made by consensus and crimes punished in a just and equitable manner. You couldn't go to the police as there were none.

They would take things into their own hands—that was control, a payback system. For example, if I was to shoot one of your family members and kill them then you would feel obliged to come back and kill one of my family members. It seldom got out of control. They had ceremonies every now and again, called Ye-Wam,[1] where they would agree to stop their fighting and get together very early in the morning. One party of the warring parties would meet at a certain place. They would light a fire, allow the smoke to ascend and that would be a signal for all the warriors to meet. They would exchange gifts equivalent to tens of thousands of dollars. They would agree to stop their fighting. They would keep their word—until someone blundered.

Other customs included cutting off the tip of a person's ear to prove their innocence. If they bled freely, they were considered guilty.

Language

There are about 300 languages spoken in West Papua.

There are about 17 different languages within the Dani family of languages. The four of which I became familiar with included Southern Yali, the Grand Valley Dani, Lower Grand Valley Dani and the language we mainly worked in—Western Dani or Lani.

The Lani language usage started at the northern end of the Baliem valley at Pyramid and extended through the Bogo valley, Toli valley, Yamo valley and right through to the Ilaga area. The Lani tribe is the largest tribe of the wider Dani language family.[2]

Within the Western Dani or Lani there are a number of dialects, but the language is still understandable over a 120 km wide area.[3] There were similarities in the Dani language family but there were

---

[1] Ye-Wam: Ax Pig – a ceremony where they would exchange axes and pigs, a binding contract for peace.
[2] Small tribes within the family like Hupla, Wano, Walak etc. were usually confined to their own small valleys.
[3] The Western Lani couldn't pronounce the letters s or c, f, h, j, q v, x, z.

many major differences between each language. The Yali would speak some of the words of the Grand Valley Dani, yet there were many other words that were totally different. If you got two people together from the different Dani tribes they wouldn't understand each other. It was a family of languages.[4]

They were a proud people who resisted foreigners coming in. About 60 years before missionaries arrived in the area one government expeditionary patrol had to shoot their way into the Baliem valley. The Dani warriors blocked them off and indicated to them they would kill them if they went any further. One person was killed and finally they let them through.

The Spiritual movement started in the western end of the tribe at Ilaga, spread through the highlands and finally reached a place that missionaries had called Pyramid because there was a rock formation in the shape of a pyramid. That is where use of the Lani language finished and the Grand valley Dani started. The local name for Pyramid was Penokwaalo, (which means half a snake).

One side of the pyramid the people spoke the Western Dani or Lani language and the other side they spoke the Upper Baliem Dani language.

There wasn't any written language at all prior to missionaries entering the area. When we arrived, we were given notes that had been written up by missionaries who had arrived a few years earlier, a sheet of phonetics which taught us how to say a few phrases and a sheet of paper with just a few sentences such as 'I want to buy this thing' or 'What is this item called?' or 'What is your name?'.

I mostly learnt the language by listening to the people whereas Betty had printed notes to learn from. Betty learnt by the notes and hearing whereas I learnt just by hearing. I picked up the everyday speech but it didn't qualify me for Bible translation since I didn't know the phonetics and the grammatical structure of the language.

---

[4] Just as English, German, Dutch, Frisian, Swedish and Danish are part of the Germanic language family.

When we first went there we had a page of phrases which we would read when we'd go to the market to buy vegetables. I would always carry a notebook and pen in my top pocket and whenever I heard something I wrote it down to help me figure out how to use it. Later, we learnt the Western Dani language to a certain extent.

Another missionary, Dave Scovill, wrote a book called *The Amazing Dani*.[5] You could speak their language, mispronounce it or use poor grammar and they would forgive you. More often than not they got your meaning.

Cowrie shells were the currency and had been so for hundreds of years, adding value as they were traded into the interior of the island by men brave enough to cross war boundaries.

They worked all day for a real good cowrie shell. You could value the cowrie shells by the wrinkles and shoulders on them. It got to the stage where I was paying two cowrie shells for a day's work.

We went along with the economy that was in existence as best we could, trying to be fair and equitable. The economy gradually changed over to rupiahs.

Clothes and Market Stalls

In the early days of the ministry we were also involved in supplying clothing to the local village folk. But supplying clothing to people who were still illiterate became an issue.

When factories produce clothing of different sizes they attach labels to indicate the size (S, M, L, etc.) but the Lani people had no knowledge of this practice. So they would have to first try on each pair of trousers or each shirt personally.

We used to trade items, run little trade stores, trading clothing, soap and essential items people would ask for.

It soon became obvious that we had to train some of the local boys to handle clothing stalls. Some were successful but most of these quickly failed as a boy's relative would come and by applying cultural

---

[5] *The Amazing Danis* by David L. Scovill, Xulon Press.

pressure, would say something like, "You are my "son," (even if just a distant relative) so you owe me." The sales boy would often capitulate and give him the article for nothing.

Chapter 4 - First Posting Mamit

During the first six months in the Toli valley we went to a new ministry area called Mamit where we built our house. This was a mountainous region only accessible by plane from the coast. We didn't have electricity. We had a kerosene fueled refrigerator and used a wood stove to cook on.

I had only been in Papua for about three months when I came across a girl who had lost most of her foot. I was told that an evil spirit had eaten her foot. What had really happened was that her foot had got infected and it must have rotted away so they believed that the evil spirit ate it. This kind of belief and medical incident was common in my time in Papua and it wasn't long before dealing with such incidence became regular occurrances.

First completed Mamit house

I met with an old lady when we first went to Mamit. I think she had heard the gospel when it had gone throughout the area like wildfire. She knew she was dying so I used to go and spend time with her but I didn't know enough of the language to fully present the gospel to her. I remember asking her if she was afraid of death, and she said "Yes." I could do nothing to allay her fears.

John McCain and Dave Martin built our house. At the same time three grass huts were built along the air strip for the workers. These huts were made of round timbers and bamboo. But we used the wrong species of timber and it rotted very quickly.

We had heard about a timber called in Lani, "appe." When we went to fetch timber for our house we thought we'd got the correct kind. We took long poles to support the house but they rotted within five years and had to be replaced. However, we heard the timber in the next valley didn't rot quickly. They used the same tree, it had the same name, but was from a location about six kilometres away.

Later on, I found out more about this interesting appe tree. If you split it while still green it would rot like an ordinary piece of wood. But if you let that tree mature and fall of its own accord, after all the foliage and bark rotted away the logs would often last three generations and would be reused in the subsequent building or rebuilding of houses. The preservation process could take about 30 years. Once they had been naturally preserved these logs could be used for posts to build the houses upon. As these logs were in the jungle, where it was often wet, shrubbery and undergrowth would grow over the logs.

Our house in Mamit rotted quickly, and after five years we had to rebuild it. When we rebuilt our house we were able to get some of this naturally preserved wood and added another preservative by using creosote mixed with used oil, the creosote also helped to stop termites travelling up into the house.

Chapter 4 – First Posting Mamit

Nggenane (Frank) in front of his house in Mamit

Building the Airstrip at Mamit

As well as building our house we worked on the airstrip. Because of the geology of Papua there are many earth tremors and strong earthquakes. There were often landslides; some steep mountains became almost bare because the quakes caused stones to be dislodged and roll down the steep slope.

Long before we arrived in the area, perhaps hundreds of years earlier, there had been a major earthquake near Mamit. This resulted in a huge landslide and it carved out a basin more than a kilometer wide in the Mamit vicinity. The central area of the basin was suitable for a sloping airstrip. The ridge of the basin to the north of Mamit was called Nggenane. So we built the whole of the airstrip, the mission and the school area on top of this landslide.

At the bottom end of the airstrip was a hill that needed to be leveled. It was 100 metres long, six metres high and approximately 30 metres wide. This hill was all dug away by a thousand or more people working on it daily for several months.

Over the years many more earthquakes were felt at Mamit. Then in April 2013 there was another massive magnitude 7 earthquake just to the north of Mamit. Boulders the size of cars came crashing down the mountain on the southern side of the Mamit basin leaving deep craters a meter deep in the ground. Thankfully those boulders missed

Building the Mamit Airstrip 1961

the government school by a few hundred meters but sadly 17 people throughout the wider area died.

We got our drinking water from a spring seeping out of the ground near the top end of the airstrip. The Lani people also used to drink from seepage springs like this one. We had to be careful about pigs foraging above our spring and of dead frogs in the drinking water pond. At another place a woman had died, they buried her on the mountain side just above a spring; the water became contaminated and could not be used for drinking any more.

We had the airstrip completed by the time of our first annual mission conference in April 1961. But because it had not yet been officially approved we travelled on foot back to Karubaga for the conference which was about a ten-hour walk.

After the conference, pilot Betty Green, who was one of the founders of Mission Aviation Fellowship, (she had been a war time pilot) walked with other missionaries from Karubaga to Mamit in order to see if it was safe to land on. Since there were no soft spots or other hazards discovered, MAF pilot Bob Johanson flew and landed the first plane on the newly completed Mamit airstrip on the 21st of April 1961.

He then returned to Karubaga and flew my wife Betty, myself and our baby back to Mamit, along with food supplies and other possessions. Just before our wheels touched-down on the sloping Mamit airstrip a down-draft dropped the plane below the airstrip level. There was a four to five metre drop off at the bottom end of the airstrip. We could have easily crashed straight into that but Bob Johanson pulled the plane to full power and turned toward the open valley. We went down valley, then turned back and landed. If we had crashed we could have died.

A similar wind related incident occurred later when returning from another conference after Desley's birth. This time the pilot was John Gettmann. Near plane crashes seemed too frequent. Later a wind curfew was applied to the Mamit airstrip prohibiting landings after 10 AM as wind gusts were too unpredictable after that time.

Another time while we were flying a pin came out of the carburettor linkage and the plane revved to full throttle. Our pilot could not adjust the speed of the engine. He couldn't shut down the engine slow enough to land safely. So, we had to fly further away to a larger aerodrome at Wamena. Then the pilot turned the engine off and glided in—known as a "dead-stick" landing.

When we opened Mamit airstrip on the 21st April my wife was already well pregnant with our second child. We were in a remote place. Then Betty woke me on the 1st of June 1961 at 3 o'clock in the morning. She said, "Frank, I'm in labour." It was dark, there was no transport, there were no other missionaries there, no doctor, there was no nurse, so I delivered my own baby.

I had to get up and light the stove, boil the water, sterilize the linen, get the scissors, everything, and go over to the medical hut and get some pain relief. Sometime between 6:00 and 6:30 AM I delivered Desley, our first daughter.

We had an old crystal radio, and we actually had to take one crystal out and replace it with a different one to change the channel. We could hear the pilot calling to us but we didn't have time to change the crystal before he went back to his own channel. Then at 6:30, the radio came on again with their regular check up on all the stations and called us. We had the correct crystal in this time and they said, "Sorry we can't come in today, we will have to come in tomorrow." I replied, "Don't worry, the baby was born this morning between 6 and 6:30." The baby was due on the 21st of June but she came on the 1st of June. We had intended to fly to the Sentani airport, then on to Hollandia where there was a big hospital for the delivery.

I called a local woman after the birth to come and help but we couldn't communicate very well due to my lack of knowledge of the language. I had to massage the fundus to stop the bleeding. Thankfully I was able to stem the flow.

The placenta was held to be sacred as it nourished the baby. If not disposed of correctly, the Lani people believed that the baby would be inflicted with some sickness or premature death later in life.

Chapter 4 – First Posting Mamit

Two of the chiefs, Tuan and Andugum, came because they were good friends of mine, and took and disposed of the placenta and blood. They said, "She was born here, she is one of our children." (It will never change, even though she is here in Australia, her family is here, she is still one of them as far as they are concerned.)

MAF pilot Dave Steiger flew into Karubaga and picked up a nurse, Pat Dale, along with her 1½ year old daughter Joy, and flew them into Mamit just a few hours after Desley's birth.

One morning, a year or so later, I prepared breakfast. We usually reserved some fresh goat's milk for baby Desley. That morning I accidentally swapped the milk we used for us adults with Desley's goat's milk. I took a spoonful of the goat's milk and was violently ill for the entire day. The goat had developed serious mastitis. That accident in swapping the milk most certainly providentially saved Desley's life.

Desley about 4

The children learnt the Lani language before they learnt English. They would chat away in Lani. We would go out and use the Lani language incorrectly and the children would say, "Daddy, you do not say it that way, you say it this way." Or "Ah, Mummy, you do not say it that way, you say this."

It took me quite a while to learn the language well enough that I could preach the gospel. I had the advantage of the linguistic work of other missionaries in the Toli valley (called by the Dutch—the Swartz valley.[6])

The children loved helping, they were a good bridge between the Lani people and us because they would go out in the afternoon to visit the women and help dig their vegetables, then go to the women's homes and enjoy the afternoon meal, which was usually sweet potatoes and greens. Then they'd come home around meal time but didn't want any supper because they'd already eaten.

My local name in Mamit was Nggenane. They named me after the big ridge just to the north of Mamit. They called Betty, Kagikwe, (assimilated from two words, Kagi and Kwe) she was named after a little valley on the west side of Mamit called the Kagi. The word "kwe" meant woman. So she was literally the woman of the Kagi River.

Our third child Heather was born in Karubaga, on 29th of July 1963. A missionary doctor, Jack Leng, and his wife, Fiona had recently arrived from England; they helped take care of her birth.

I became part of the Lani legend of how the gospel came to the Lakes Plains area. The legend was that somewhere in the future, a foreign person was to come into the area, and teach the gospel and they would hear the word of God. I decided to walk out to the area, across the mountain range, with a group of men with me. One

---

[6] People thought Swartz meant dark and that the valley was named after the colour of the people's skin, but it was actually named in honour of the German who funded the Dutch expedition in 1920. The Swartz valley was locally known as the Toli valley, the name of the river flowing through it.

night we slept on a sandy bank of a little stream at the foot of the mountain. When I was trekking there would always be about 20 Lani people with me, some carrying my goods. One of the boys from the house would come with us. We would sleep by the trail. One nice clear night as we were laying there asleep, no blankets or anything, just nice sand by a stream, at 9 o'clock this boy jumped up and started jumping around yelling out, "It's gonna rain, it's gonna rain, it's gonna rain." We told him to go back to sleep and let us sleep."

Even though the sky was clear, he kept saying, "It's going to rain."

An hour later, he jumped up and started again with "It's gonna rain, it's gonna rain." We told him again to go back to sleep. About

Heather

midnight, the clouds gathered on the mountain, they gathered and gathered, and the sky looked menacing. The thunder and lightning started and it rained like mad. We could see the little stream rising and rising.

Some of the older men who were with our group were wiser than us young fellows. They had crossed the little stream and built a little bivouac to sleep in on the knoll of a hill. All of us crossed over the little stream except for one man who stayed with my goods. Then he took my goods up to safety. The little stream rose up, up, and up, completely covering the sand bank that we had been sleeping on. It came up and covered the little knoll with about three feet of water. The water rose above my knees. We had to just wait there, dripping wet, no way of making a fire or anything until the sun came out so we could dry ourselves and our goods.

The river finally went down enough that we thought we would cross back to the other side. There was a big tree there, they chopped the tree down and built a kind of bridge across the river but the flood waters picked the tree up and carried it away. The people told us not to worry, that the locals would see the wood chips on the water and come looking for us. Sure enough, those folk did come up looking for us and we went down to their village for the next night.

So, a part of the legend was that someone would come in a storm, and so what happened to us seemed to fulfill their legend.

I was once asked how high the flood waters rose. They flowed through the swamp around the trees, about two meters high.

In 1920, a Dutch expedition had travelled up the Idenberg river (which later was called the Mamberamo.) This river met up with the Rouffuer river and included more than 50 kilometres of rapids. The expedition crossed up into the mountains, walked into the Toli Valley and set up camp. The expedition included carriers, cooks, and islanders, many of whom were conscripted from prison.

They trekked on through to the Grand Valley in central Papua. Then returned on the same track coming back home about a year later. When they came back, they brought back dysentery. More than half of the local people perished. If someone got sick they would go off to the bush and they would live there in self-quarantine, separated from the others. That's how many remained alive because they stayed away from the infection.

I wasn't aware of the death toll till I got there and talked with the older men. They said, "Look at us: we are all that is left of our play mates the others died of dysentery, we are all that is left." There were only a few of the older men left.

When the exploration team crossed the mountain range, at about 6,000 feet up, they then went up to the top of Doorman Top (at about 11,600 feet) and put some stakes in the ground. Those stakes were still there in 1971 when I went with another missionary, John Dekker, and my son David. We climbed to the top of the mountain and had a look around. The timber was rotten but the place was still identifiable.

When the missionaries came in they started a Christian school at Karubaga as a witness in the area. They would ask each clan to send in a husband and wife to be taught so they could communicate the message and get the message right. We arrived in Karubaga when the school had just started. We had to learn the language, preach the gospel and teach them.

Ministry in Karubaga

A missionary with the Christian and Missionary Alliance mission, Gordon Larson, walked with some evangelists from Ilaga through to Pyramid—well over 200 km on the trail—going from village to village, preaching the gospel. He slept in huts when he could or in the open. He had a bad knee and was always in pain but God enabled him to continue walking until He eventually healed him.

Most of the young teenage boys learnt very quickly. We had to put up a building, we used slabs of timber to make desks to write on and benches to sit on. Betty would oversee the schools, she made sure they had pencil and paper and all the primers. Education spread throughout the valley very quickly that way.

For people who have never held a pencil in their hand we had to have a preliteracy program to get the people used to holding a pen or pencil, making controlled marks on the paper. A two-year-old Australian child would grab a crayon and draw on books and sometimes the walls. But the Lani people and their children never had

The Bible school at Karubaga is where we moved from Kanggime. Later it was moved again to Mamit. The one at Mamit became the main centre for the whole valley. Kanggime means place of the dead.

that option. They called paper—banana leaves.

It wasn't long before outlying villages wanted a school too. A Lani evangelist and his wife, a medical worker and his wife, and a teacher and his wife would go to a new station somewhere and open it up. The people—particularly those out in the Lakes Plains area—asked to be taught. No sooner had the teaching begun that the next-door tribes would say that they wanted to learn the gospel too.

So, church leaders had to look around for another team of teaching evangelists, medical worker and his wife, etc. It kept snowballing like that. They had a very minimal wage. The church would give a huge offering once a year to help the local evangelists and we supplemented clothes and other things from our station.

Every morning, before the people went out to work, we would have 1,000 people come and sit on the airstrip to listen to a message of the day. That would happen five days a week. I would tell them a message. They would then go out to work and pass on that message

Yambuk and Wara were two of the first cultural missionaries to leave Mamit and learn another language to spread the gospel. They went to Kamur near the Krongkel River.

so every day, they would saturate the area with what I taught.

I then started teaching the elders in a Bible class situation; they would go home on the weekends, and preach what they had heard. They would talk in their huts at night about what they were taught.

Instead of the legend stories they used to pass on now the gospel was spread. They had no Bibles to start with. We started producing notes and those notes would be put into lessons. We would duplicate them with an old spirit duplicator and we would give the notes to them. We would get the notes, and I would read them. Then gradually I got to expand on those notes as I learnt more of the language from the people, got help from the notes and learnt the proper way to speak the language.

Other missionaries started translating passages of scripture. One missionary translated the gospel of John. The people just loved it. Other New Testament books followed, then the Lani New Testament based on the *Good News Bible* was officially published in 1982 by the Indonesian Bible society.

We started up a Bible study group in the Lani language. That developed into a proper Bible school at Karubaga where we sent ten couples each year. There they did a two-year course learning the Bible. A lot of them later became evangelist missionaries.

One example of the difficulty of translation and how one's own experience can get in the way was when I was attempting to translate a message from the book of Amos. Amos was a herdsman from Tekoa. I was brought up on a farm and my experience was with cows. I thus accidentally translated herdsmen with reference to cattle rather than as shepherd.

The missionaries working on Bible translation from the Old Testament initially just translated accounts—creation or other stories that stood out. For many years these stories became the people's knowledge. Most of that was styled like a children's book, not a careful verse by verse translation. Finally in the late 1980's and through the 1990's those missionaries started to make a serious attempt on an accurate verse by verse Bible translation. The translation committee started with Genesis and worked right through to Malachi. Once they finished the Old Testament they went and revised the New Testament, then in 2009 the whole Bible was published.

Due to the gospel I saw a big transformation with regard to the payment of the bride price and the fighting that had accompanied the process. The clan that was receiving the bride paid the equivalent of tens of thousands of dollars to the father, mother, brother and it seemed everyone related who came out of the woods to claim some. They used to fight about it as it would be paid out over a period of time rather than at the initial ceremony. One clan would say, "Give us more money, we want more money." And the others would say, "Sorry, we don't have it." They would then pick up their bows and arrows and start to shoot or punch one another. One person got killed during one event I observed.

I said to the people one day, "What is the cause of your fighting, your killing?"

They thought and they said, "Bride Price." Then they stopped it.

One of the main uses of the cowrie shells was for paying the bride price. When they moved to the rupiah, when the cowrie shell

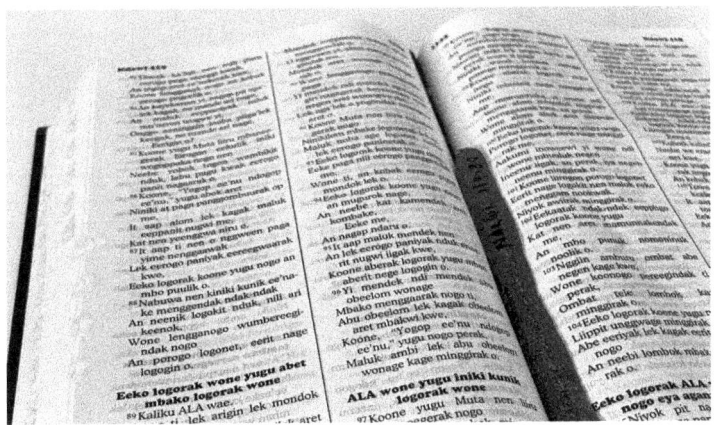

Lani bible opened to Psalm 119

was no longer used, they lost a huge amount of wealth. This they accepted amazingly well.

Another clan who had obviously had a grievance with the clan we were with came in one morning and sacked the village. An old man named Gegola who had problems with his knees was unable to escape. They tied him up and would have taken him hostage. The clan had enlisted the help of numerous other confederate clans and hundreds of warriors armed with bow and arrow and stones took the village. I was determined to rescue Gegola so I hopped on my usual mode of local transport—a 90cc Honda motorcycle—and sped through the human blockade. Because of the speed of the motorcycle and because they respected me as big chief, they did not fight me and so I was able to rescue Gegola. This elderly man was of great assistance in our work because while the younger locals readily accepted the gospel there was much resistance amongst the older folk. Gegola was able to convince many to accept the gospel due to his seniority.

This is where we taught people how to write. Many of these people had never seen a pencil before, so the first step was teaching them how to control it.

I was a practical person. Though I didn't do much with their activities they would help me with the garden, make paths and construct little bridges over streams. One time a very strong man named Lenwarit wanted an axe or parang (machete). He offered to carve a footpath along a rocky cliff face going down toward the Toli River to Panaga. He used (and wore down) my crowbar which was made from a driveshaft from an old '26 Chev car.

I was doing evangelism and teaching the leaders. My wife did medical work. She also taught the people to read and write. She would work with the people on community development, a better diet and teaching them how to look after the animals. She taught the people to grow different sorts of crops and different vegetables. They would invariably sell them back to us. I taught them how to build, do carpentry, how to sharpen a saw and to use a hammer etc. I found the work so rewarding! I loved the people and felt at one with them.

When we first went to Karubaga we had a kerosene operated refrigerator, quite an ancient one, given to the field, and it came to the

Clinic

point where we had to defrost it. Inside the freezer there was a pool of water which froze like a dish. We were cleaning out the fridge and putting the things into the sink. There was a girl there who used to help Betty do the housework and after a while she was hunting for this glass dish. She had put it in the sink and it had disappeared. She wondered who had taken it. She had put it in hot water in the sink so it had melted. No wonder she couldn't find it.

When Dua, a young Lani fellow who had been like a son to us, had tried to handle a bull from some yard somewhere the bull stepped on him, and squashed his ribs. He just couldn't get better. He just sat in his hut waiting to die. I asked the Lord to heal him. A few days later he was walking around. He later became a schoolteacher.

A man wanted to kill us a year after we were in Mamit (we were praying for him). We said, "you are going to be healed. The young farm boy (Dua) who is like a son to us, he is healed. You are going to be healed too." The people thought we were going to supply them with all sorts of riches. They had not yet grasped that God offered them everlasting life and spiritual riches, not material things. We had

Lani ambulance (stretcher bearers)

been at Mamit for over a year, nothing happened, so this fellow and another Lani from down in the valley way were the leaders in trying to stir up the people to kill us because we hadn't produced the goods. We didn't know about this plot at the time. I went away on a trip down in the valley and was away for several nights. Betty was home with a couple of babies, and at 9 o'clock at night, she heard this voice outside, "Kagikwe, (Woman of the Kagi river) I'm going home now." Betty just about leapt out of the house. She didn't know anyone was out there. A fellow said he was out there to watch in case anyone had come to kill her while I was away. Later this man and I became good friends. His name was Tuan, the father of Dua (the man who got trodden on by the bull). The leader that wanted to kill us and I became friends later on. He later died.

Betty with David, Heather and Desley setting out on a trek

Chapter 5 - Resistance of the Yali Tribe

The Grand Valley Dani considered themselves to be the people of the centre of the earth. They were "The People." They regarded themselves as the "head" of the tribes. The other tribes were merely the "tail," so because the Western Dani had accepted the gospel the Grand Valley Dani said they were not going to accept it.

Stan Dale was a pioneering missionary.[7] Whereas Mamit was only a day's walk from our other mission stations at Karubaga and Kanggime, Stan wanted to open a totally new work far to the south amongst the Yali tribe. He decided to carve out an airstrip in the Heluk valley at Ninia—and it was grueling work. The local Yali men were not interested in helping move rock and dirt to level out enough ground for the airstrip so Stan had some men come from Mamit and Karubaga to help.

Stan Dale was older than us. He had particular ways of doing things which people found difficult at times. I had nothing bad to say about Stan Dale—but he was different.

When he was a commando during the war other soldiers would sometimes have a rest period in the afternoon and go to sleep but to keep himself fit Stan would put a 35-pound pack on his back and run up to the mountain top and back down.

I think he may have been autistic. He had a terrific memory, an analytical memory. He would analyze the history of the American civil

---

[7] *Lords of the Earth,* Ron Richardson, Regal Books, 1977. See also *Ninia,* Joy Dale Crawford, Beracah Book Publishing, 2016.

war, he would say, "Why didn't that general do this and why did he do that."

He once gave a history lesson about an American civil war battle at a mission conference with American missionaries. Some of those missionaries had come from that area and he described the battle and how the troops were deployed. Stan had delved into the history of the town and the military conflict there, which these missionaries didn't even know about. He was an amazing fellow to work with—at times a little difficult—but amazing all the same.

At Ninia he had to carve out the airstrip, build a temporary dirt floor hut for the family to live in, learn the Yali language, preach the gospel, do Bible translation, build their house—and trek out to other villages to preach. Spiritually it was a hard area but by 1966 a small group of people had become believers.

Then a couple of local Ninia men decided they wanted to go and preach in another area about a day's walk down valley from Ninia. The Yalisili people were traditional enemies of people in the Ninia area. Both men were killed which led to Stan going to investigate and then he too was shot with five arrows. Overnight he walked back to Ninia and barely survived.

One of the unwritten laws of the highland tribes was that if a tribe fed a man then no one else from that tribe could kill them. Some of the Yali however resisted the gospel so vehemently that they broke this law. The local people were intent on killing the missionaries to keep the message out of the Seng valley. They didn't want the message in the valley so were intent on killing him next time they saw him.

Stan was fearless. Even though that first attack on his life required several major operations, after he had recuperated he was ready to go straight back to the ministry. During the next two years Stan worked on translating Mark's gospel into Yali, making a small hymn book and continued discipling the Ninia Christians.

At one point he even cut up 20-liter steel drums for those trekking with him to use as shields or chest guards.

Chapter 5 - Resistance of the Yali Tribe

Then in September 1968, Phil Masters (whose ministry was at Korupun, two weeks walk past Ninia) and Stan decided to trek from Korupun to Ninia to check out tribal boundaries and see if there were suitable places to build another airstrip.

They had been walking for seven days. They would walk until it got dark and stop for the night. On the last day, the people from the hostile villages began following them and threatening them all day. Phil and Stan went into a hut and an old man called Kusaho came along and offered them food. The food was very welcome as they'd been walking for a week and rations were starting to run down. They got potatoes, which was mostly for the carriers. They had four local carriers which meant that according to the laws of the tribe they were welcome, they weren't to be touched or harmed.

However, the warriors were intent on killing them. The next day Phil and Stan went on their way, walking parallel to the fairly swift Seng River which had vine bridges over it. Their Lani carriers wanted to cut the vines and let the bridges go so the tribesmen couldn't pursue them. They decided however not to do that. As they went up into a gorge the warriors crowded in on them.

First of all, they shot Stan with dozens of arrows, and killed him, then about 30 meters further on, they killed Phil Masters. They chopped up their bodies and took them away and had a feast. They distributed their flesh throughout the mountain area.

When the carriers, who were just up ahead, saw what was going on, they hid in the undergrowth. Then they dropped whatever they were carrying, ran for their lives and escaped. One of them got lost in the jungle and we never heard from him again. We assume he perished somewhere in the jungle. The other three reached help at other places.

Stan and Phil died on 25 September 1968, eight years to the day after we arrived in Hollandia. Stan was just 52.

I had heard that they had started an uprising against anyone not of their tribe. They said they wanted to force all strangers—police, army, teachers, nurses, missionaries—from their valleys. They gathered a lot of support around that area and up into the main valley and Grand Valley.

About five weeks later we went with some soldiers and they attacked us, but they weren't any match against the guns of the soldiers. The warriors thought they were invincible because when Stan was alive he would set off firecrackers and the enemy would back off. But this action made the enemy believe they were immune to bullets. This is why when the government patrol had gone in years earlier the Yali warriors went up on a ridge and threw their chests out as if to say, "Shoot us if you can, you won't kill us." However, several of them regrettably were killed. Later we had heard that seven men died.

After the deaths of Stan and Phil we asked the people to meet with us. One of the Yali men from Ninia who knew Lani translated what they said for me. Quite a few people gathered together. They said, "Oh no, it wasn't us that ate the missionaries, we didn't kill the missionaries or eat them, it was that tribe over there."

That tribe was going to come over and join them and wipe us out. They were vehemently denying any association with the killers until an old woman said, "We all ate them. We all joined in, we all ate them, you, me, the kids, we all ate them." All the men that were there looked downcast and looked at the ground, so we knew she was telling the truth. The carriers that were there with Phil and Stan identified some of the warriors.

There were many bones at the attack site by the river. They chopped them up by the river and carried the body parts out and had a feast elsewhere. Later on we visited the place where the warriors had their feast and gathered up all these bones which had been cooked. There were quite a few bones left over from the two of them.

Later there was some confusion over what I believed to be Phil Masters' jawbone. I was sure that some of the remains were that of Phil but when I communicated this to his relative via a bad telephone line there was a misunderstanding as they thought I referred to his teeth as having been "filled" but rather I said they were Phil's and so they did not accept that these were his remains.

Because of our Lani evangelists, the gospel did eventually penetrate the Grand Valley tribes. In the 1960's anthropologists and missionaries estimated there were about 90,000 people in the Baliem Dani, with another 120,000 Lani people. Those figures have now more than doubled.

Chapter 6 - Tragedies and Trials

On 31st December 1968, the same year Phil and Stan were killed, we were attending the funeral of Vida Troutman who had been a long-term missionary with Christian and Mission Alliance CAMA. The funeral was held at Wissel Lakes. While at the funeral we were informed of a MAF (Mission Aviation Fellowship) plane going missing.

The Newman family had been on holidays staying with a family on the south coast and were returning by plane to Mulia in the highlands. On board were Meno Voth the pilot, and Gene and Lois Newman who were bookkeepers for Mission Aviation Fellowship and their four children.

The plane flew over the jungle swamps. The pilot intended following the big Baliem river through the mountains up to Wamena but because of the low clouds he ended up following the wrong river.

They were in the wrong valley—a very tight valley, the same valley where Stan and Phil had died. The plane crashed. They were all killed except for the Newman's son Paul who was only ten years old, one year older than our son David. When the plane crashed the little boy got out of the plane and managed to find his way to the village. An old man called Kusaho, the old man who gave food to Phil and Stan before they were killed, met him and kept him for three days in order to protect him. Some of the people wanted to kill him. The old man said, "No, you can't, our laws say you can't because I gave food to his father."

Despite the language barrier, whenever the boy cried the old man asked him what he wanted. Was he thirsty? He gave him some water from the spring. The old man then assumed the boy was hungry and cooked him some potatoes. He then lit the fire to get the boy warm—all to no avail. The boy still cried because he had just come out of the plane that crashed and all his family were killed.

When we couldn't contact the plane, we had to get a helicopter from PNG and fuel to try and locate the missing plane. The second day was too cloudy to see anything and flying was dangerous but a desperate and dangerous search was still undertaken. Next morning fog covered Wamena though it was clear on the ground. Hank Worthington flew through to Wamena. The pilots had a radio schedule with each mission station to check for weather conditions. Other stations in the Baliem valley were also fogged in but the answer from Pyramid was that they had clear skies.

It is dangerous to take off in fog at any airport. But Wamena is especially risky as it is surrounded by mountains. Pyramid was only 18 miles to the northwest from Wamena. High mountains surround the valley all the way around except for a very narrow river gap to the south. There was no GPS or other navigational aids in those days. There was also a 300-foot-high hill going transverse across the landing approach just 3½ miles from the Wamena airstrip.

In 2009 a commercial cargo plane tried landing at Wamena in fog. After the first attempt to land led to a go-around they tried again but with fog they did not have the airport in view. They were about 300 meters off the centreline of the airport and hit that hill. The pilots and four others died and the plane was totally destroyed—it became metal confetti. Only the cockpit, wheels and wing tips of that plane were still identifiable afterward.

Back in early 1969 with the Wamena airport fogged in the MAF pilots were desperate to find Menno Voth's missing plane. They undertook an extremely dangerous take off. They decided to fly at a set rate of climb and on a set direction for a specified time. If they did not fly into clear weather then they planned to return to

Chapter 6 – Tragedies and Trials

Wamena airport on the exact rate of descent and a compass heading 180 degrees from the initial direction. Once into clear air there were several other small airstrips they could land at. (MAF regulations today would not allow such a dangerous action.)

In spite of this first attempt, poor visibility did not allow us to see anything. After three days we were able to get into the crash area by helicopter; we landed in the valley adjacent to a bridge.

Hank Worthington, the head of MAF and I were at the crash site. We were extra careful because of the hostility just shown to Phil and Stan. Hank was standing on the fuselage to see over the scrub and saw two men coming down the path on the other side of the river. When they were near the bridge we saw Paul Newman climbing over the rock. They were bringing Paul back to us after hearing the helicopter. We then knew they meant us no harm. Paul went back to the US to live with his maternal uncle.

Chapter 7 - Communicating the Gospel

Many native people groups of the world have a legend of the flood or salvation. The Lani were no different. They had a legend that way back in their past they had eternal life but the human race had lost it. They believed that somewhere along the way the truth had been corrupted. There was a contest between a snake and a bird as to who would bring them the message of eternal life. Because the snake shed its skin every year so that it always looked new they believed the snake never died. It just lived for ever and so it had the secret of eternal life. The bird on the other hand could fly quicker than the snake could crawl but the bird worked against the efforts of the snake to subvert and prevent the snake's message from being delivered.

They thus had a belief that some strangers would come and eventually bring them the secret to eternal life. (Note the similarity of the bird and the birds who snatched away the seed in the parable of the sower, Matthew 13:4, 13:19. Note also the serpent who appears wise, telling Eve half-truths. Legends often get corrupted as they are passed down, Genesis 3:1 and 4.)

In this case the serpent became the truth teller and the bird the thwarter of truth. They also had a legend about a dispute over fruit (analogous to Eve's eating of the forbidden fruit and the dispute similar to Cain and Abel's offerings).

The first missionaries who learned the Lani language had to find a concept in their language to communicate the idea of spiritual eternal life. As they listened and learned the legends of the Lani people the legend of the snake and bird finally gave them the key. Nabelan

Kabelan, literally meaning, "my peeled off skin, your peeled off skin," described the material physical everlasting life that the snake, who they believed physically lived forever, was trying to bring to them.

When the Lani people heard missionaries use this term they recognized that it was the missionaries who were the strangers in their legend who would bring them the message of everlasting life. It was a very material eternity: they believed that they would never get sick, they would never die, that their pigs would always be nice and healthy and everything would be just rosy. That was their concept of eternal life to start with.

To compound matters, western influence had created what was called the cargo cult. The cargo cults started off in the Pacific Islands during the war when the American planes came in bringing all kinds of goods. They thought "Ah, we want to be a part of this." And they would get all these goods. This spread right throughout New Guinea. Another missionary and I went out to the Lakes Plains area. He set up his base near the foot of the mountains where a river would drain out to the big river and then would go out to the ocean. The cargo cult thought this position was logical because water always flows downhill, flows out to sea. His name is Macris, so they changed it to Macristos. My name is Clarke, so in that area they called me Clarkam. So I became a part of the legend, the cult legend.

Between the cargo cult legend plus their legend we had lots of work to correct the misconceptions. Initially their understanding was like legalistic Christianity.

They could recite the Ten Commandments. They could recite the crossing of the Red Sea, and things like that. Eternal life to them was that you never die, you never got sick. Animals never die. Pigs were their currency. If you had pigs, you were considered rich. Their gardens had nice big, sweet potatoes. It was like a revival without the life. It opened the way for us to preach. It took a while to teach them, to get the message through.

As the gospel was spread, the Holy Spirit began to work in their hearts, gave them a more spiritual understanding of the gospel and they became believers. It was a mass movement of mostly whole families, not just one person. The unity of the family was extremely important in the Lani culture. Here is one example: I heard that when a particular chief died, eight members of his family committed suicide as an act of love and respect—so it was with the reception of the gospel. A man would not come alone, the whole family would have to be there, and all of them were baptized together. They would talk it over and decide they were going to accept the Lord as their saviour as an entire household. They would all wait till they had unity as a family. If a man came to me I would suggest he wait for his wife; then they would all want to be baptized together. If we felt that all the family understood salvation and the fundamentals of the faith then we'd baptize the whole family.

To baptize the people we totally immersed them in a stream, lake or pond. The people were very precise about full emersion. If a part of their body was not immersed—such as if they had their

Baptism, done by Jacques Teeuwen and Frank. One of the first baptisms at Mamit. That day we baptised over 600 people.

elbow up or their head wasn't completely immersed—they felt they were not baptized properly. It was very legalistic for a long time. We had to correct this error of course. After having been baptized I saw them put a hand full of water on their heads to make sure they were properly baptized.

Initially, because of their material understanding of everlasting life if someone got sick after they were baptized the people would think that person wasn't baptized properly and that was the reason for him getting sick. Because no Christian had died there for several years they also thought that baptism meant they had physical eternal life. When Christian people finally died the people wondered if they had been baptized properly. Finally, with correct teaching, they understood that eternal life referred to spiritual and not physical life.

In fact, almost the whole of the adult population made a confession of faith and were baptized. We expected that a big percentage of people would fall away but only one or two fell away of that generation. The people who turned from their old ways said, "We are going to stop fighting." They had big gatherings together and they burnt their bows and arrows. They burnt everything so they couldn't

Baptism at Kuwari

fight again. They made a big pile about 20 metres long of bows and arrows and the women added charms with which they used to practice sorcery. All these things went on the fire and were burnt. That cleared the deck as it were. It was hard to get rid of the idea of material/physical everlasting life completely and unfortunately it still exists amongst some to this day in spite of our efforts.

The Lani people were zealous evangelists and whenever they heard the message they had to go and tell someone else. They needed little encouragement or prompting from the western missionaries. Once they heard the good news, they eagerly wanted to spread it far and wide.

They started fanning out, going north from where we were, out into the Lakes Plains area, where there were 17 tribes. They went to the Eastern highlands amongst the Yali people, and the Kimyal and they went to the south coast, amongst the Kayagar, Asmat and Sawi peoples, the region where Don Richardson (the author of Peace Child) worked.

Frank and Betty, 1985

Frank and Betty with first bible class

Chapter 8 - Daily Dealings

During our early years we were allowed to have .22 caliber rifles but eventually the government took them off us and kept them. Then, they let us have them again for a few years.

One time in 1963 I was in a canoe on the river with some Lani people. I shot a snake out of a tree. The Lanis thought the snake was going to fall into their boat so they jumped into the river—which upturned the canoe—so the snake and I were separated. They cooked the snake but I didn't get any as I ended up in a different canoe from the snake.

Once I stayed in a hut by the river which was infested by fleas. Deserted Bausi houses were thick with fleas. One needed to keep two meters or more away when walking past. There was a platform about 90 cm above ground. The legs were black/brown with fleas; you could run a hand down the legs like a squeegee. I found a fallen tree which went right close to the hut. I tried to walk along the fallen tree to dodge the fleas.

There were lots of scary times such as when I was with Dave Martin in a canoe amongst swirling current in Rapids. Another time a croc hunter's canoe was caught in a whirlpool; he jumped on to a rock as the canoe went to the bottom. An oil company search in Rapids resulted in the chief geologist's drowning and the project was aborted.

One time I was travelling up the Mamberamo river in a dugout canoe with outriggers like a house boat with space to sleep. The boat was covered by large mossie nets as there were millions of mosquitos.

Many would get in under the net before nightfall and stay until daybreak. It was powered by a 40 HP Johnson outboard motor.

Once, Bogo was about to jump into the river to defend Costas who he thought was about to be attacked by people at the rivers edge. They were carrying gifts of sugar cane but from a distance he thought the sticks of sugar cane were bows.

Later we made trips in a boat with a 350 HP Pakajet Packard V8 motor which swallowed petrol by the gallon! We travelled right up the river to where the Yamo river entered the system. We found large round rocks. We picked up several and took two back to Mamit. There is still one in the guest house (Frank's house in Mamit) to this day.

One time, Bogo was sitting on the front of the boat plumbing the depth of the river. The motor quit in mid stream. The boat threatened to follow the side current and drift down past an island or wash up on its beach. I looked over the side of the boat and found a main rib of sago palm frond that I was able to use as an oar/paddle to keep the boat from harm until the motor could be restarted.

In the jungle we had a lot of encounters with all kinds of creatures including death-adders, crocodiles, Papuan black snakes, flying foxes and great flocks of pigeons. Tree kangaroos were also plentiful and were a great source of food. Wild Balinese cattle would cause havoc at night, wrecking gardens. People would set traps to try and catch them.

There was a story about something that lived in the Lakes Plains, it was huge, lived in the water and came out sometimes. They say that they would see it go through the rubbish and regrowth at the edge of the lake; they saw a pathway where it would wriggle its way through. I never found out what it was. I think it would have had to have been a huge snake like an anaconda or something like that. There were also stories of dinosaur-like creatures in the Lakes Plains area.

I bought snakes from the people. They weighed about 20 kilograms. One snake would spend its life in the trees, wrapped around branches, his underside was much shorter than his top. So, when you laid him on the ground, he looked like a Z because his

CHAPTER 8 – DAILY DEALINGS

belly skin was much shorter than his backbone skin. People would kill snakes and I would buy them and feed it to the chickens—they would lay eggs like mad. The people ate snakes, but I didn't eat them.

There was once a man at Papasena with croc teeth punctures

Lani man chopping and cooking pork with stones and wood for lunch for guests in Tolikara

across the top of his upper legs. He was paddling his way along a river when he disturbed a large old croc. His wife was in the canoe with him. The croc attacked them. He described how its lower jaw was under the canoe while its upper jaw was on the top. He had crouched down to sitting position so the upper jaw went over his upper legs and left two rows of punctures. His wife was at the rear of the canoe. She had an axe but was too scared to move. I don't know how he escaped. I saw him about two weeks after the event and he was making a good recovery.

In West Papua, the most game thing I ate was cat. It was a domestic cat that had gone wild out in the jungle and grew enormously; they strapped it on a pole like a pig, brought it in and paraded around with this huge cat. I also ate Sago grubs although I didn't fancy them. I ate them cooked. They'd find a sago tree, split it open and would then count the days by tying a knot in a piece of string every day. They wanted the grub at a certain stage so they'd count the number of days—10 or 15 days—and then it would be ready for eating. They knew how to do that precisely, very accurately. I tried eating it although I thought that I wouldn't like it—and I didn't like it.

There was acceptance of the gospel, although they became legalistic—do this, do that, don't do this. From area to area they have a saying using words that had a different meaning. They had rules outside the Ten Commandments—such as 'you shall not break any green things,' which means you don't harm the green things on a Sunday. Anyway, I used to go along paths from village to village, there was always nice tall grass. I would pull the centre out and eat the soft pith of the grass. They would castigate me for doing this, because I was bringing the message and yet I was still breaking one of the Ten Commandments. It took me a long time to realize just what they meant. In their language everything was taken literally. You do not do gardening on a Sunday.

Chapter 8 – Daily Dealings

Idioms changed from area to area in the Toli Valley. They'd have an idiom that if you took the words literally you'd get a different meaning.

Another commandment was you shall not have intercourse with a woman out in the garden. However, what they meant was immorality—immoral people going out in the jungle or garden, that is, not necessarily husband and wife. What came through to us is that all sexual intercourse had to be done in their hut. It took a long time for us to work out what they were talking about. And all it meant was don't go out philandering in the garden.

One highlight of my missionary work was a testimony of a man who was like a father to me, called M'buru-m'buru. I would call him "my father" and he would call me "my son." I just had that kind of relationship with him. He and his wife were such a loving couple! As he got older he stopped working; he would sit around my yard and look after the ducklings. The ducklings were taken away from their mother when they hatched and they would grow up in the yard. A lot of people would stand around my yard; some with sores on their legs. The sores would attract flies. Then the little ducklings would come up behind them picking the flies off their legs. Sometimes people would step back and step on the ducklings and squash them. So, this old man would sit there and watch, to make sure the ducklings didn't get squashed. I could see that his health was failing.

When our daughter was born we went away to Karubaga and about four days later some men came from Mamit to Karubaga to tell me that this old man had died. Then we went back to find out the story from the missionary nurse. She told me that he went back to his hut one afternoon to eat the afternoon meal and he said to his wife Eregu, "Eregu, please hurry up and cook the potatoes, I'm going up to be with my Father." He went over and sat against the wall of the hut and became unconscious. The missionary nurse went over and made him comfortable and then he passed away. It's a story that stuck with me—he was a man who never learnt to read and write although we tried to teach him to read; we finally worked out that he had old eyes, (perhaps cataracts) he couldn't see the letters. Still, he knew the Lord and followed him.

While I don't usually believe in dreams, one dream I had seemed to be a God given encouragement. After we'd been in West Papua a few years I had a dream one night. I was preaching in the Lani language and it gave me confidence that I could preach fluently. I normally had to have an interpreter. I would read the story and someone would translate what I was reading in their own language. This dream spurred me on to keep learning and trusting the Lord for His help.

Meredith was born on the 14th of March 1971 at Karubaga, assisted by Elisabeth Cousens, a missionary doctor, and Jessie Williamson, a missionary midwife. It was not long after this that we were sent north to the Lakes Plains area.

Andugum was one of the most godly Dani men I ever met. He wasn't the brightest man. The others objected because he wasn't smart. But he was faithful to the end, went preaching. He is shown here with his wife Kimikigwe.

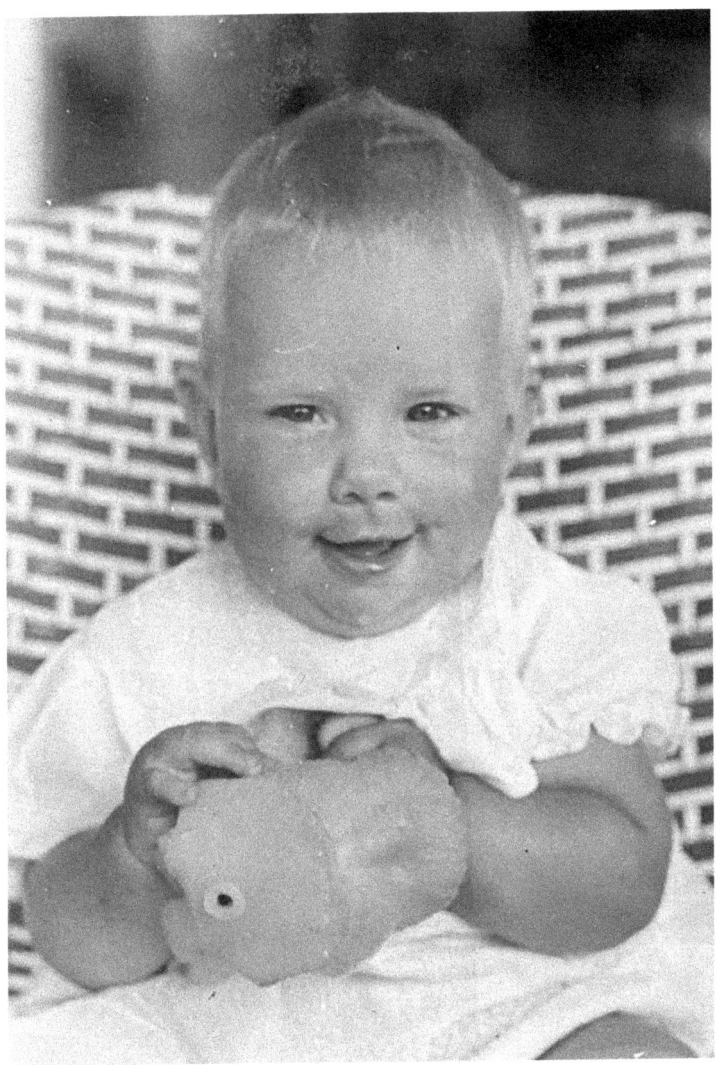

Meredith about 8 months old

Chapter 9 - Our Second Post

In 1971 after 11 years at Mamit we were sent north by the mission conference to the Lakes Plains area to help with the logistics of the rapidly increasing Lani mission effort. This was a swampy region only reachable by plane. To each one of the Lakes Plains areas we sent a Lani evangelist and his wife, a schoolteacher and his wife and a medical worker and his wife.

They needed support: they needed two-way radios, they needed air transport, materials for teaching, supplies for medical work, etc. We supplied the logistics as much as we could. We opened the airstrips in each new area as it was needed. We arranged flights, supplied medicines for their health, maintained two-way radio communication, supplied teaching materials and whatever else we could help them with. Initially, the two-way radios were powered by 12 volt car batteries. We'd have to deliver these to the stations and pick up the old ones for recharging. Eventually we were able to obtain solar panels and regulators to charge the batteries on site. We had the ministry of logistically supporting these native evangelists for many years. Depending on the terrain, local transport within the region was either on foot, by 90cc motorcycle or by motorized dug-out canoe.

When we moved from Mamit to the Lakes Plains area we had a little bark hut literally made of stripped bark from the jungle—two rooms and a little alcove at the front. That's where we had the wood stove. People from over the river who didn't know much about us came in and they saw Betty go out to the aeroplane and get a tray of eggs. Then one day they saw Betty cooking at the stove and the pressure cooker making a noise as it got up to steam. She opened the pressure cooker and got out a chicken. Oh! That's what she did with the eggs! They thought that she put the eggs in the pressure cooker and out came a chicken.

One of the tribes in the Lake's Plains area was the Undergoom. They had a lot of beliefs regarding evil spirits.

One of the things that the Undergooms told us about evil spirits was they used to rely on them to give them directions so that the days pig hunt would be successful. So the night before hunting they would sleep out in this special place amongst huge rocks with space between them and there the evil spirit would tell them that they could go and get some pigs tomorrow or don't bother going as there won't be any pigs. They didn't actually tell me that it was reliable but the way they told me sounded like it was reliable.

I did hear of an incident where they did see an evil spirit: a couple of young men were walking around at nighttime and they saw some apparition go through a certain hut. It went over the hut then went into the hut and at the same time a woman who was in the hut screamed.

On the edge of the river at Lakes Plains there was a bank on one side that dropped down about 15-20 metres with a layered piece jutting out into the river. The layers had split so that it looked like some kind of animal with its mouth open and it was believed that was the evil spirit that ate children.

I had a rifle and just for fun I was shooting at an old tree. An old man named Ngalikali thought I was shooting the evil spirits. It would have been better if I hadn't done that but I suppose being young and due to lack of knowledge I just did it. The man was elderly and died soon after. He was a sworn enemy of the Undergoom tribe.

Even though they made peace with the Lani people the Undergoom wouldn't pass over to the other part of the river into this other territory. Even though they made peace with the Lani people he still didn't trust this fellow.

The Anggen Kunik (seed united) was a secret name that every warrior had. Every warrior had their own secret name. In extreme danger, they'd call on this secret name to give them deliverance.

Amongst the Babarwar people there was a belief that if a woman had twins then one of the twins was fathered by an evil spirit. They'd leave the "evil" twin to die on the bank of the river, often just covering them with sand. The Lani missionaries would find them and save them. They loved babies and couldn't get enough!

"Magical" ceremonies would be performed to bring judgment or retribution upon a person. I did not delve into this much but tried to discourage them although because of the secret nature of such ceremonies we did not always know when people were practicing them. Occasionally we'd see the remains of a ceremony such as the remnants of a fire and certain stones which would have been heated in the fire.

That was their beliefs. These beliefs changed once the gospel came. It was a big change that took time. As they were taught more of the gospel they would forget about these things.

Unfortunately, many of these spiritual beliefs remained long after missionaries such as John Dekker thought they had been forgotten years earlier. For many years they held syncretistic beliefs until they really matured in the gospel.

Typical Lani village

Chapter 10 - Vet, Surgeon, Dentist, and More

Not only did we have to correct misconceptions about spiritual eternal life but we also had to correct many misconceptions about illness and recovery. When the people became ill with a lung condition such as a cold or the flu they would believe that they were struck by an evil spirit. This became the term, "I've been hit by an arrow."

The Lani people believed when a person died that their spirit would come out and live in a tree or in a rock somewhere; if you were an enemy it would take its vengeance out on you. Another belief is that a person would be able to transform themselves into another form such as a bat or flying fox, travel hundreds of kilometres and terrorize the person living there. We had a case where a girl had her first baby; she was clawing at the wall of the house thrashing and carrying on. Unfortunately, the baby died at birth. They believed that was to do with the suitor who wanted to marry her first. She had rejected him and married someone else. They believed that the former suitor transformed himself into this evil spirit to terrorize her with a vengeance.

It was believed that some women had powers that could be used for vengeance on someone if they wanted to. Did they really have power? I believe it was autosuggestion. They believe that it could be seen in their eyes.

The people of Papua had a very old practice called blood letting. They say the blood gets up into their stomach and goes mep (or dark.) They use a little bow and a little arrow, about 300 mm long, with a 3 mm point on the end, and a wad of stuff to stop it going in any further. They would shoot a vein in their leg which lets the blood out. It's called a mborluwap. I was fascinated with this practice—no one died and it didn't seem to do any harm if they felt better afterwards.

My wife Betty would teach the younger men to help clean wounds, how to bandage them and look after them. They didn't have bandaids or bandages like we do now; they used old torn up sheets and would wrap it around wounds.

Betty would teach the young fellows how to dress wounds and give injections; they became quite proficient. Eventually they registered as clinic helpers and were paid a wage. Finally they were recognized by the Indonesian medical system as competent medical workers.

There was one person who had been burnt on his legs. He just sat at home. Because he hadn't been exercising his joints his legs locked up in one position, he had lots of scarring and couldn't walk. So they had to carry him on a stretcher wherever he went.

Another man was seriously burnt due to an accident involving fuel. He had collected both petrol (Avgas) and kerosene (Avtur) from different planes after a pilot had checked for water in his fuel tanks, and then mixed it together in his kerosene lamp. It exploded and he suffered serious burns. After being in hospital for quite a while he sat at home and his knees started to lock up. Once he started to exercise, he got some of his mobility back.

Miscarriage and spontaneous abortion were common among a small proportion of women. Premature babies often did not survive because they were too weak. Often shortly after a loss the women would become pregnant again. Because the mother was worn down from the prior pregnancy the next pregnancy would often result in the same loss. Betty would help these individuals by giving them advice about not lifting heavy items and to assist them with vitamins and better nutrition. Betty's assistance resulted in many such women having successful pregnancies and births.

Because of a lack of protein, lactating mothers and their young

Chapter 10 - Vet, Surgeon, Dentist, and more

children would develop a reddish tinge to their hair. To remedy this, we introduced a more protein rich diet including a particular variety of sweet potato that had double the protein of the common variety.

Several times we had to remove embedded objects such as arrow points which had broken off in the flesh. The Lani did not use barbed arrows; their arrow points were designed to break off in the flesh. They would cut a groove around the tip of the arrow 3.5 to 4 inches back from the tip to aid it in breaking off on impact. Invariably infection would set in and over time a tough cocoon type growth would seal the arrow point off from doing further harm to the body. Sometimes it would stay in the body inert but activity could cause the tip to break through the cocoon and travel further into the body.

When a wound opened up again we'd attempt to pull it out using long forceps. Sometimes this was impossible, and we had to just let things take their course. Sometimes this would result in death. One of the pastors there had an arrow tip in his chest for a long time. A group of people were holding him up above their heads (being very happy to see him), much like one would hold a ball above one's head. This activity caused the arrowhead to dislodge and it killed him.

One woman jumped over a fence and was impaled on a stake which we had to remove from her leg.

There was widespread use of a particular leaf similar to pennywort which they'd place over an open wound to keep the flies off it or put it on a boil which was forming to help it to come to a head and burst. As western-trained medical people, we looked on that practice with scorn until we were actually able to identify the leaf and verify its medicinal properties. The Lani name for this leaf was kimbiengga.

One time there was a man who was involved in a fight. His opponent slashed him with a razor-sharp bush knife inflicting a wound in his back about 200 mm long and about 50 to 60 mm deep. He sat with the wound facing the fire so the flesh dried up and became crusty as if it were half cooked. He was flown to our base for treatment, after which for fear of the locals he promptly got up and walked all the way to his home village.

There were times when I would have to extract teeth. There were people who had teeth that were rotten and painful. The only way they could extract them was to put something under it and wriggle the tooth for a couple of days till it was loose, then we could get it out. I thought I could do better than that. We had proper forceps and due to the tooth being so infected, the gum being infected, the tooth being rotten, it was better to just pull it out.

When we had to extract a man's teeth, two of his friends would come along with him. One would hold his legs while the other one held his arms against his body and I'd just pull the tooth out without any anesthetic. One time a fellow came in and I asked, "Which tooth is it?" and he showed me his tooth. So, I pulled the tooth out. The fellow came back five minutes later, and said, "You pulled the wrong tooth." He'd come back to get the proper one taken out.

A young man had been chewing betel nuts which were very hard. Betel is a mild narcotic chewed with lime which can eventually cause oral cancer. He cracked the shell with his teeth. One tooth became very painful. It was a molar and we couldn't see anything wrong with it but we found out it was snapped off just below the gum. Sometimes when we had to get the tooth out we would leave the root behind so we would have to use root forceps and dig down to get the root out.

One time, a woman had given birth. The umbilical cord was still attached, it hadn't been cleared properly. They pulled the cord and in doing so they pulled the uterus out of her body. This poor woman was lying there, waiting to die. I didn't know what if anything to do so I got her to go outside and lie on a grassy patch with her legs high up and I pushed the uterus back in. It stayed in; she had babies after that.

Chapter 10 - Vet, Surgeon, Dentist, and more

Not only did I help people, I was also a missionary vet. If there was something wrong with an animal, they would call me. I was called up one day to a place called Wamena, a big city in the interior. A fellow had a cow with a calf and the uterus came out of the cow; it was a huge uterus. With the cow lying on her stomach we were thinking, "How are we going to get that back in," well we finally got it back in and she had live calves after that.

I would also give people injections. There was this disease called yaws framboozia which was a very contagious skin complaint. They would pick it up in their skin and it would go all throughout their body and if it was left in the body long enough the tibia would bow and quite a few different things would happen, other deformities would occur. We used a medicine called penicillin with aluminium in oil. One injection given daily for five days would clear up mild cases of yaws framboozia. I would carry a box of this medicine and would inject it into the people as I went past.

I went to one place, and there was this girl who was about 16 or 17 and she was covered in sores. Nobody wanted to marry her because she was covered in all these sores. So I gave her an injection. Then about a week later she came back and said she wanted to work alongside my wife; she became a house help. She was healthy and clean and wanted to work. Previously we only kept young men as house help; we didn't mix men and women helpers together in the yard and in the house. She soon got married and had children.

There was another young man who came there one day when I was at the Bible class. When I came back Betty said to me, "Come and see this man." Here he was, covered in these sores, he had a huge sore on his chest, many scabs and it had gotten into both eyes. His jaw had changed shape, his teeth were protruding, one ankle was frozen so he had to walk on tip toe. He was a mess. Because of his complaint he was so smelly that he had to be in a hut of his own. They would take the food out to him. Finally he came in to be treated. We had to have him stay around for a lot of treatment so we gave him a job cleaning up the garden. Then we could give him an injection every five days. Unfortunately, the deformities stayed, but the sores finally cleared up.

Eventually, the government medical staff came through with a program to examine everyone for yaws and treated everyone. They gradually got it under control.

There simply wasn't the missionary man-power to help everyone with every illness. Many missionaries had multiple tasks. My wife was a nurse but she was also a house wife, mother and teacher. We were all very busy from dawn to dark. We got up early in the morning to do our devotions but the earlier we got up the earlier we were disturbed. After we had our evening meal several people would visit, sit in the living room and just talk. We'd all have a cup of tea.

Once a year they would have a big offering for the local Lani missionaries. They would offer money, fruit, vegetables, clothing, etc. Occasionally the fellow who collected the money disappeared into the city to spend it. Once it was gone, it was gone; the police weren't interested in catching thieves from another area; no one would track him down. Thankfully this didn't happen very often. When we first went to Mamit steel was very much prized. But, if we happen to leave a steel axe on the ground and forgot about it no-one would steal it.

Chapter 11 - Evangelism in Lakes Plains

We didn't get involved in the teaching or learning of any of the languages in the Lakes Plains area.

I always spoke with help from the Lani missionary that worked there and he translated into the local language. We had no way of checking how accurate his communication of the message was. He had no way of coming back into the third language (Indonesian) that we knew. After we had come home from furlough I went back to one of our mission stations and spoke in Lani to the Lani missionary there. The missionary in charge knew the local language and relayed the message back to me in English. It was quite accurate. I had no way of checking any of the others.

The evangelists carried the message far and wide through Papua. They were very zealous to spread the gospel that they had received. God had his quiver full of these polished arrows! The men used different arrows for shooting birds, pigs, fish and humans. Analogous to the Lord using the term fishers of men, Lanis had a concept of an arrow to catch men via the gospel. This made me think of Isaiah 49:2 "And he hath made my mouth like a sharp sword; in the shadow of his hand hath he hid me, and made me a polished shaft (arrow); in his quiver hath he hid me."

We moved out to the Lakes Plains area where there were many tribes; Lani evangelists went into each one of those places. If I wanted to communicate I could use a Lani interpreter and they would translate my message. I never actually preached to many groups out in the Lakes Plains as there wasn't the opportunity to do it that much—except for the occasional baptism where I would give a short message. As a result of the mission work amongst the Lani tribe they themselves became the streams of life-giving water to the thousands of people in the surrounding islands.

The Lani preached far and wide. They decided to go throughout Indonesia, to all the islands. One young boy was taken by the government to a place called Ternate to be trained as a civil servant. He was a Christian. While he was there he started to witness. Many were converted and he started a church. Wherever Lani went they took the message with them. Several families would go into an area, would start a meeting and they would witness. They said they were like worms. They worked under the soil, they worked out of sight but you saw the results with the conversions. They went right throughout Asia. Their goal was to start in Jerusalem, up through Europe, across to England, then to America and then down to Australia. After going right throughout Asia they would join up in Jerusalem again to complete the circle. That was their vision. They had this vision the remaining time we were there and even after we left. This vision continues to this day. So far they have travelled to many of the islands of Indonesia, taking the gospel and making many believers.

Some of the miracles they told of were that they would pray all night over dead bodies and by next morning they would come back to life, be all right, walk again. These stories were told far and wide. These stories were not confirmed.

The Lani men were part of the rescue mission after the 2004 Aceh tsunami. They were amongst the few that were willing to put on gumboots, go into the mud, retrieve rotting bodies and gave them a decent burial. They helped the people get their villages back to functioning.

It was fantastic how the Lord had this tribe in mind. There was a great turning to the Lord; they were great evangelists. I just had to admire them they were so terrific. They were wonderful, truly lovely people.

The Christian message and ethics became the normal part of the whole society. It was rather a bit rigid to start with.

They wanted me to become the big chief. I could have been the king chief. All the tribal chiefs referred to me. I didn't accept that position. I kept right in the background, pushing them. I just went there to tell them the gospel and let the gospel work its way out through their thinking and actions—so that they would govern themselves using those values.

Listening to the gospel

Chapter 12 - Later Years

The United Nations managed the transition from Dutch to Indonesian control from about 1962-1963. In May 1963 the Indonesian government was in control. They appointed administrators from Jakarta but in the early days it was up to the missionaries where we should go and what we should do.

When Indonesia took over control the new Indonesian language came into use; under the new government the people's culture changed. Prior to this many schools only taught up to about grade 3 primary. When the Indonesians came, they brought the full spectrum of education: primary, secondary, and tertiary education. It was supposed to be free but it ended up costing a lot for them. The parents recognized that their children needed education. They would work hard to provide the wherewithal for their children to go on to secondary education. They had to leave the area to go to high school which was set up by the Christians who supplied teachers. Otherwise they only went to grade 6. So, if they wanted further education they had to live in the area where the high school was.

The parents would give everything they had to keep their children educated. These days some of them are doctors and professors. Some went into parliament. The present governor of Papua is a Lani from Mamit. Others got a TV station going. Another man was doing road works with bulldozers and excavators, building roads. They would make long bridges over rivers, then they'd seal the roads. They paved the airstrip in Mamit.

I went to Mamit, John Dekker went to Kanggime and Dave

Martin was at Karubaga. For some reason the people held us in high esteem. We three men were "the apostles" to the people in our area of ministry. Other missionaries laboured harder and more diligently, yet they didn't gain the same esteem because we were the initial "strangers" of their legend who brought them the message of eternal life. I imagine that when I die I will become a part of their legends and the myths will grow. There are already myths about me up there. When I die I'll be St. Frank and the legends will continue to grow.

I was in West Papua from 1960 to 1985. After four years I came home for a year. We were sent far and wide on deputation and I was separated from the family quite a bit. While I was travelling the children had to stay with their mother, especially after they started school. This caused problems later in life. On one occasion, I was away for a long time and my eldest son began to identify with his mother more than me. He became very close to his mother because he didn't have me there.

In 1990 when I went back to West Papua for a visit I learned of the legend of the River Women. A woman was talking about her boy.

Ministry in Doyo Baru Sentani, Papua

He was about 1 year old and would incessantly cry with a high-pitched scream. He was mentally very backward due to brain damage. The story went that when they went out to the garden they would have the baby in a net bag which was his bed, and they would hang the bed on a stick while they did their gardening. The river women allegedly came up and would leave their brain damaged baby and take the good one.

Nggenane Frank Clarke senior missionary in interior Papua for 25 years

They believed that there were spirit women who lived alongside the rivers; they were evil. They would steal babies. Or if they had babies of their own they would swap their babies for a better one. When the first missionaries came into the area they were all men. The story went that these men would go at night and visit these river women—these evil women. These women could make a person go insane. A man was taken down to these river women and they made him go insane for quite a few months. This seemed to fit the imagination of the people and they believed this story.

In the early days I'd gone over to the other part of the valley to make a canoe for one of the children. There was a full-grown man who seemed out in another world, and the people said that he was a child of one of the river women. That's where I first heard of it but it was only on this latter visit that I understood the meaning.

In 1999, when I was visiting, at a remote airstrip there was quite a squabble going on. This fellow came around the corner to see what

Family waiting for airplane to take them to school at Lake Holmes (Lakes Plains area Danau Bire)

was happening and he walked straight into the spinning propeller of a commercial twin engine plane. He was killed. No one saw him walk into the propeller, they just saw him dead.

My first wife, Betty passed on in 2015. We were married for 56 years.

Frank preaching Karubaga 1989

Karubaganwa preaching

Chapter 13 - My Last Visits

Frank with Lipiyus and Governor Lucas at Mamit 2016

In 2016 I made a trip to West Papua unknowingly with a serious infection in my foot which only became apparent once there. On my return I had two toes amputated.

Frank with Lani woman mourning the death of Betty

Chapter 13 – My Last Visits

I went back to Papua again in 2017 to be amongst the Lani people. I was encouraged by their progress. One of the teenagers had achieved an education and become a government contractor. He was building roads, bridges and airstrips. He was putting bitumen on the roads to make them more durable. He started a gold mine. He hired contractors to sell the gold. He hired a helicopter and he used to go in and take food into them and gather the gold and bring it out.

That gold mine was at the sand bank on the mountain side where I'd once slept. When I went up there in 2017 they took me up the mountain by helicopter and also took me up to the site where they were sluicing the soil and extracting the gold. It amazed me that I was at the place where I'd slept back in 1963 in that storm.

On Sunday the 24th of December, 2017, I ended up at government hall. I didn't yet know it but I was to be the preacher. The head of the church that we set up was the preacher but he deferred to me, he pointed along the row to the person next to me but when it was time to get up it was me. I only had six minutes to get my message ready so I preached from the book of Romans. They gave

Frank teaching at Mamit on one of his later visits

me a translator who spoke excellent English and knew the Indonesian language well. He was very quick. I would say what I was saying and he would translate it straight away. He only hiccupped on one word which wasn't in their language and I said that they would have to put it into their language. The word was, I think, "smithereens." At that meeting there was a young fellow from the Lani tribe who had gone to a seminary in Java and after three years he married one of the local women from Papua. They had a little child called Gideon and he came back from there on his own to Papua with the stated intention of providing food for his father, such as rice, and fish for Christmas. However, his real intention was to come back and commit suicide.

He came to the meeting I spoke at about three hours early. He sat on the grass outside, waiting for the meeting to start. He really didn't know why he was there. When the meeting started he came inside. I spoke on Romans 8:9. I said, "If any man have not the spirit of Christ he is none of his." That hit him like an arrow and made him realize that he wasn't a believer. He became a believer there and then and went back to his wife. He didn't tell her what had happened but she said, "What's happened to you, you've changed." She kept querying him on what had happened. He didn't tell her; he just let her guess for a while. Later, when I went to Jakarta, they came to the little hotel where I was staying and I was able to lead her to Christ. We had Bible readings every morning while we were at the hotel and it was there where I was able to lead her to the Lord.

Someone once asked a person what the greatest hindrance to God working powerfully through the tribal culture? The other person replied, "It's a missionary." It's because you get in the way, you can divert the emphasis on where it's going and put the kibosh on things, which you shouldn't do.

The Lani people developed their own liturgy. They didn't sing like us; they had three notes they sang and when one of their people would give a verse of scripture whilst preaching, expound upon it, then they would turn it into song. By singing it the people would learn

Chapter 13 – My Last Visits

it. Some other missionaries translated English songs into Lani and got the people to sing them but it was never the same. It wasn't their language. Their language is the mother tongue. That is the one they are hearing. A foreign tongue—even though they might understand it—it doesn't have the same effect as the mother tongue.

I believe that in the training of missionaries both anthropology and genealogical background should be covered and used in their field of service. This is so that the missionaries understand who is related with whom.

My 2017 trip was cut short due to the same recurring infection causing the need for amputation in 2016. This time I required debridement (the medical removal of dead or damaged tissue to improve the healing potential of the remaining tissue.).

In 2018 I met and married my second wife Astrid from Indonesia.

I travelled to West Papua for the last time in 2018. Due to deteriorating health since then I have continued my ministry via regular internet live stream.

Conclusion

As I reflect back over my life I can't help but think of the words penned by J. Grant about God's polished arrow from Isaiah 49:2. "This verse describes a prophetic description of the Servant of Jehovah, whom we know to be the Lord Jesus Christ. Speaking of His preparation for service, this Servant declares that "he hath…made me a polished shaft; in his quiver hath he hid me."

The process of preparing an arrow involved polishing the shaft until all roughness had been taken away. Before a battle great care was taken to ensure that each shaft in the archer's quiver was polished to perfection. All unevenness was removed and all cause of imbalance eliminated. This was a task which was not accomplished in just a few moments. Skill, patience, and determination were required to ensure that the arrow was perfectly prepared and would not deviate from the course on which it had been dispatched. It would be effective in penetrating the body of an enemy in a clean manner. Without the polishing process the arrow would be of little value in the battle. It would miss the mark and possibly injure a friend or ally. However, when polished to perfection there was no more effective weapon in the hands of a competent archer." [9]

I feel this verse describes the process by which the Lord prepared me for service in West Papua and also prepared each of the Lani missionaries who became polished arrows in God's quiver that were

---

[9] "A Polished Shaft (Is 49.2)" by J. Grant., *Believers Magazine,* July, 2007. http://www.believersmagazine.com/bm.php?i=20070701 accessed on 15 May 2023.

sent out into all of the surrounding islands to bring the gospel to so many millions of people.

As Mr Grant goes on to say in his article:

"We need to be 'polished' so that we are effective in service. Those who seek to serve the Lord are aware that this is necessary. The elimination from our lives of all that would damage our ability to serve the Lord effectively must be a prime consideration. The question facing us is whether we have the desire to do this."

As I look back over my life, and reflect even on those early years, I can only marvel at how God prepared me for His service. From my difficult times as a child, to my study of nature, and my work in the bush, were all key to what God had in store for me in the river regions, valleys and jungles of West Papua.

The polishing process is at times painful. There is a personal cost to allowing God to take off our rough edges and polish for Himself an arrow which will hit the target. God only has imperfect people to work with, but it is our willingness and submission to Him which makes us fruitful even in our frail state of humanity. It is amazing how God can use even the weaknesses in our character, and the things which others, and even we at times think are thorns in the flesh, to His glory. May we give ourselves to the master archer's service for only He knows what He can do with our lives for His purposes.

Postscript
(by Joseph Stephen)

Frank Clarke was called home to be with his Heavenly Father on 29 June, 2023 at the age of 89. At his memorial he was remembered for his dry wit, his generosity and his long service to the Lord. His contribution to the Kingdom of God will live on in the lives of the Lani people. His humour and generosity will be remembered fondly by all of us who are left behind. As I wove the threads of Frank's notes into these memoirs I did my best to capture the essence of all that he told me first-hand in a series of interviews and social chats over a period of about three years. Let me finish with Frank's own famous words, "if you want it done rougher than this, then do it yourself."

> For My Memoirs
>
> "Hardships often prepare ordinary people for an extraordinary destiny"
> C S Lewis